HOW TO WRITE
AN EFFECTIVE
CV AND COVER LETTER

STEP-BY-STEP WRITING GUIDE.

LIDIJA SIMUNOVIC

Copyright © 2022 by Lidija Simunovic

Edited by Tajana Marinovic

All rights reserved.

No part of this publication may be reproduced, distributed, or transmitted in any form or by any means, including photocopying, recording, or other electronic or mechanical methods, without the prior written permission of the publisher, except in the case of brief quotations embodied in critical reviews and certain other non-commercial uses permitted by copyright law. For permission requests, write to the publisher, addressed "Attention: Permissions Coordinator," at info@linkinglines.com.

Table of Contents

1. THE PURPOSE OF THIS GUIDE 4
2. THE VERY FIRST STEP IN CV WRITING: GATHERING INFORMATION 5
2.1. WHAT ARE YOUR SKILLS? 7
2.2. THINK ABOUT YOUR WORK HISTORY 8
2.3. EDUCATIONAL BACKGROUND, COURSES, AND TRAINING 10
2.4. COMPLETION OF THE FIRST PHASE OF CV WRITING 11
3. THE ACTUAL CV WRITING 14
3.1. TONE AND STYLE OF A CV 15
3.2. DOCUMENT DESIGN AND LAYOUT 20
3.3. WRITING CV SECTIONS 26
3.3.1. BASIC INFORMATION 26
3.3.2. WRITING A PERSONALIZED AND HUMAN-FRIENDLY CV 27
3.3.3. FLEXIBILITY OF THE CV STRUCTURE 29
4. THE OPENING SECTION OF YOUR CV 31
4.1. TONE AND STYLE OF THE OPENING SECTION 35
5. SPECIFIC CV SECTIONS 36
5.1. PRESENTING YOUR WORK EXPERIENCE 39
5.1.1. TONE, STYLE, AND KEYWORDS IN WORK EXPERIENCE DESCRIPTIONS 41
5.1.2. PRESENTING RELEVANT WORK EXPERIENCE 46
5.1.3. PRESENTING RELATED WORK EXPERIENCE 48
5.1.4. PRESENTING UNRELATED WORK EXPERIENCE 50
5.2. PRESENTING YOUR EDUCATIONAL BACKGROUND, COURSES, AND TRAINING 52
5.2.1. PRESENTING EDUCATIONAL BACKGROUND, COURSES, AND TRAINING WHEN SWITCHING CAREERS 55
5.2.2. PRESENTING EDUCATIONAL BACKGROUND, COURSES, AND TRAINING WHEN YOU HAVE RELEVANT WORK EXPERIENCE 58
5.2.3. PRESENTING UNRELATED EDUCATIONAL BACKGROUND 60
6. INCREASE YOUR CHANCES OF SUCCESS 62
6.1. FINE-TUNING YOUR CV 62
6.2. THINK ABOUT SOCIAL MEDIA 64
7. THE IMPORTANCE OF COVER LETTERS 65
7.1. TONE, STYLE, AND KEYWORDS IN A COVER LETTER 67

7.2. THE STRUCTURE OF A COVER LETTER   68
7.3. THE LAYOUT OF A COVER LETTER   74
8. A QUICK OVERVIEW OF WHAT YOU'VE LEARNED   76
8.1. CV WRITING STEPS   76
8.2. CV AND COVER LETTER WRITING TIPS   76
8.3. JOB SEARCH TIPS   77
9. DIVE INTO JOB SEARCH (FAREWELL)   78
10. ABOUT THE AUTHOR   79

1. THE PURPOSE OF THIS GUIDE

I started a CV and cover letter writing business called Linking Lines in September 2015. Since then, I have guided and helped the careers of many people from different parts of the world.

I either provide career coaching sessions, optimize LinkedIn profiles or write professional CVs and cover letters. For those who want to invest a little bit more in themselves, I provide all three.

Throughout the years, I have gained valuable insight into the art of CV writing and job search in general, and I now want to share it with you.

This Guide will help you if you are:

- A job seeker struggling with CV writing
- A job seeker with a "generic" or "general" CV
- A job seeker with a tailored CV that does not bring results

***

There is a shorter and a longer path for each endeavor in your life. Through my work and clients' feedback, I have learned that my approach to CV writing offers a much-needed **shortcut** for many professions. In this Guide, I will share it with you and, hopefully, change your perspective on CV writing and job search in general.

I will share the knowledge that I've accumulated over the years and teach you how to write a winning CV and a cover letter, step by step.

You will learn how to tailor your CV, and by "tailor," I mean optimize it, so it brings results.

2. THE VERY FIRST STEP IN CV WRITING: GATHERING INFORMATION

CVs used to be long, tiresome lists with tons of information no one actually needs. Today, the expectations regarding CVs are quite different. For example, you don't even have to share certain information, such as your marital status or date of birth.

Modern-day CVs need to be tailored and optimized for the position you are applying to. Social mobility has brought many great things, but at the same time, you have to know that it also brought more candidates for the same job you're interested in! That is why you need to dedicate some time and write a proper CV that will bring results. Your CV should not be merely a list of what you have done in the past.

But **how** do you write a CV that brings results?

Well, first thing's first: I would recommend the very first step to be getting to know yourself.

I know that sounds corny, but once you solve this, you will be able to introduce yourself in full capacity. Furthermore, you will be able to transfer your self-awareness to your CV and present who you are to the potential employer.

I know you might wonder how to do this.

For some, this will be the hardest step, while for others, the easiest. It depends on how self-aware you are at the moment.

So, let's jump straight into it!

In order to get to know yourself, I ask you to write the following:

- A list of your skills and personality traits
- A timeline of your job positions
- A timeline of your educational background

I would recommend using an actual pen and paper. There's a special connection between you and what you write on a piece of paper, and it can't be compared with typing on a keyboard.

2.1. WHAT ARE YOUR SKILLS?

This might seem like a trick question at a job interview when they ask you about your strong points. But it is not a trick question! It is essential for you to be aware of everything you bring to the table.

Once you know this, you can start thinking about how to put it to good use in your job search and CV writing.

That is why I suggest your **first step** is writing down all your skills and personality traits.

Of course, you will not use all of that in your CV, but you need to get an idea of how it looks in writing.

So, create a list that ranges from advanced knowledge of Excel to being friendly, flexible, and approachable.

Spend at least 30 minutes thinking about your skills and traits.

***

If needed, ask others for help! It has to be someone who knows you really well on a personal or professional level (or both). However, if you decide to ask someone from work, don't make it too obvious. Try to slide it into a conversation, if at all possible.

2.2. THINK ABOUT YOUR WORK HISTORY

The next step is creating a timeline of your work history. I know it's not exciting, but it needs to be done.

You should list all your past positions, especially if you are unsure of what you want to do next.

Why is this important?

Well, maybe, you had a part-time position 9 years ago, and you now realize that was your dream job! You never know, so it does not hurt to list all the positions you have **ever** held.

Those can be student jobs, full-time jobs, temporary positions, volunteering experience, internships, one-off projects – it really does not matter! List them all.

Ideally, you will get a timeline of your adventures in professional life, but I understand if you can't list positions chronologically. This is hard if you had many positions or if you are a mature job seeker, but at least give it a try! It will make your life easier if you manage to do it.

***

When writing down the positions, make sure to include the following:

- Company name

- Employment duration
- Role title

Here's a little extra, just for you to get to know yourself a bit better – write down *why* you left the position.

With that, you will have a better understanding of your path. It is not the same if you left because you found a better-paying job or if you were fired because of poor performance.

Be honest with yourself and write the true reason.

***

How much time you spend on this task depends on your age and career path. If you've changed many jobs, it's going to take you longer than if you only had one job. Also, you need to identify the reason for leaving your job, so I'd say it will take you at least 30 minutes to complete this task.

2.3. EDUCATIONAL BACKGROUND, COURSES, AND TRAINING

After you have returned from your journey to the past, it is time to take another spin.

Only this time, focus on any formal and informal education you have received. We're talking about courses you have attended, training programs your company prepared, and even workshops and conferences you participated in.

You need to create a **timeline of your educational background.**

***

Write down the following:

- The organization that carried out the program (university, learning platform, agency)
- Month and year of completion
- Title of the program

You don't have to describe anything just yet; simply list everything.

The point is to learn what makes you tick, what you are drawn to.

Maybe you love theory, exams, and hardcore studying. But perhaps you prefer getting down to work and enjoy learning through practice. Whatever it is, similarly to the skills list and timeline of the positions, this will also reveal a lot about you.

Again, it would be ideal if you could produce an actual timeline, but it is OK if you can't.

Similar to the work experience task, how much time you spend on this one will depend on your background.

2.4. COMPLETION OF THE FIRST PHASE OF CV WRITING

The whole **point of this first phase of CV writing is realizing what you are leaning towards.**

You can learn this by observing job positions, course choices, skills you have developed, and reasons for leaving your job(s).

It really helps to see this in black and white because you become more aware of your path.

You are about to complete the first (abstract) phase of CV writing in which you are discovering who you are.

In order to do so, you need to answer this question: **what do you want to do next?**

It is not so much the question but the answer that is terrifying. Sometimes it is an honest *I have no idea*.

Suppose you **do** have a clear vision of what you want to do next – well done! Good for you! Unless you want to reassess your choices, you can skip the following few paragraphs. :)

However, if your answer really is "I have no idea," don't be scared – that is **completely fine.**

I will help you answer this question.

***

Bring awareness to the skills lists and timelines you have created.

The list of skills should be at the top, and then the work history and educational background timelines. That way, you have all the information laid out in front of you, and it is easier for you to observe what you wrote down. I would encourage using an actual pen and paper because it helps you connect with the content.

While looking at the information you provided about yourself and your history, answer these questions:

- Do you see a pattern in your work history? For example, did all your positions last 6 months? If yes, why?
- Does your educational background match your work history? Meaning, did you complete an online course in digital marketing and then worked as a digital marketing specialist?
- Did you start at an entry-level position and worked your way up without necessarily having the education for the role/field?

I would recommend you take the above questions seriously and take your time to answer them. That is the best way to assess your current situation and to identify in which direction you should take your professional life.

Once you determine which position you want, you can start the actual (practical) CV writing process.

If you want to be sure you are making the right move, answer this question as well: **why** do you want to do it?

Does it make you happy? Do you enjoy it? Are you bored and ready to try something new because you like learning? Does it pay well, and you feel like it could give your family a better life? Is it because your friends are in the field, and they told you it is an awesome gig?

You don't have to tell me; tell **yourself.** And be honest!

***

After you decide what you want to do next, you need to look into how you will do it.

And I don't mean *how* in the sense of *how you will drive a truck*. I mean, **how** in a sense, what if you have no experience in the field because you want to switch careers? *How* if you were out of a job for 10 years? *How* if you just moved to a new country?

Well, now is the time you check the skills list and timelines I asked you to compile. You need to use those to **find the best way to present yourself** to a potential employer.

Here are the specific steps you need to take:

- Write down what you want to do next.
- Find a link between the desired position and the skills list and/or the timelines you compiled.

Basically, you need to find out what makes you a **suitable candidate for the role.**

You need to either have the required work experience, educational background, or the skills needed to perform the job.

Regardless of what the connection to your desired position is, you will really want to focus on that.

***That* is your golden ticket to the interview phase.**

And once you have identified it, you can start the CV writing process.

3. THE ACTUAL CV WRITING

Let's start at the beginning. You need to open a **new** document in the word processor you usually use.

Yes, you've read it correctly. You are *not* going to download a CV template from the internet. You will *not* use a CV maker app.

You do not need that – **you** are going to write your CV from scratch!

I will recommend the document design and layout. Then, I will explain the elements of a CV so you can understand the concept of each one. Thanks to that, you will be able to decide on the best structure most beneficial to you.

Your CV needs to reflect who you are, which means you need to personalize it. And you need to tailor it to the specific job position, and I am going to teach you how it's done.

3.1. TONE AND STYLE OF A CV

First of all, we need to set one thing straight, and that is what tone and style you should use in your CV.

CV is a document used in a business, professional setting. That means your tone and writing style should be **formal** and **objective.**

Stay away from long descriptive sentences, personal pronouns, and opinions. Instead, use concise bullet points, avoid pronouns, and offer facts.

Not only does that help to get your message across, but it also helps to shorten your CV – and that is definitely something you want to do. You need to understand one thing about CV writing: **page space is valuable, and you need to use it wisely.** People reading your CV don't have all day to do it. They have loads of other CVs in their inbox, so you need to be mindful of their time.

***

If you have ever researched CV writing, I am sure you have read that you need to use an **active voice** and **avoid nouns.** That is actually true – you make a more significant statement if you openly say you were in charge of something, rather than being more of a bystander.

When it comes to **field-specific terminology and slang**, you should use it, so the readers can see your knowledge and understanding, but do not exaggerate. It is, of course, great to show that you are familiar with the most commonly used terms but do not use acronyms for absolutely everything. If your CV has to go through a recruiter first, chances are they are not so deeply involved in your line of work, so it will sound like gibberish to them. Balance is key.

Here is a **cheat sheet** to help you, together with real-life examples. The below applies to *all* sections of your CV:

- **Do not use personal pronouns** – it is not professional.

DON'T:
I have 12 years of experience in marketing, and I think my field of expertise is SEO.

DO:
- An SEO expert with 12 years of experience in the marketing field

WHY: You are not writing an essay or a review, so your personal opinions or points of view do not matter. Try to remain as objective as possible and give pure facts to your reader.

- **Avoid overexplaining and too many details** – stick to bullet points.

DON'T:

I demonstrated a great ability to assist in the organization of daily tasks and to run a busy office environment while helping colleagues with technical issues and office equipment maintenance.

DO:

- Proven ability to organize workload and run daily operations of a busy office
- Able to resolve technical issues and maintain office equipment

WHY: With two bullet points, you are saving valuable space while sending the same message. Also, you sound way more professional.

o **Incorporate keywords for the desired position in your section.** The text needs to read fluently, and it needs to make sense. Use selected keywords only if they fit the context of what you are stating.

DON'T:

Simply copy-paste the "Key Requirements" / "Essential Criteria" section into your CV:

· Self-motivated & resilient with a capacity to work under pressure and meet tight deadlines

· The ability to multi-task and manage projects as well as supporting Business as Usual activities

· Ability to work as a team player and lead a team of HR admin/HR officers

- Strong business awareness & commercial focus
- Strong attention to detail
- Competent in Microsoft Office

DO:

Take bits and pieces from the job ad & description and incorporate them into your CV in various places. Some of those key requirements might be used in job descriptions or merged with other statements you want to introduce – mix and match.

- An excellent team player with the ability to manage projects, multi-task, and meet tight deadlines
- Flexible, organized, and quick to tune in to business needs and focus with great attention to detail

WHY: If you copy-paste everything as it is in the job ad, everyone will notice it straight away. When it comes to utilizing parts of the job ad to your advantage, you need to be sure you can deliver. Always use those elements that are genuinely true and which apply to you. In this particular case, it would mean skipping the Microsoft Office part if you are not comfortable with all the apps within the package.

- **Use verbs and avoid nouns** as your CV will seem passive if loaded with nouns.

DON'T:

- Production line equipment maintenance
- Experienced in record keeping
- Familiar with project and people management

DO:
- Fully competent to independently identify issues and maintain production line equipment
- Proficient in collecting and entering data and keeping accurate digital records
- Familiar with designing, organizing, and managing projects and motivating and supervising teams

WHY: Verbs mean that you actively did something, participated in, or led an action. It gives the reader the impression that it was you who carried out something. With verbs, you're proactive; you're the doer. If you use nouns, the descriptions seem less active and less personal; it is as if you're describing someone's (or anyone's) position rather than your own.

- **Boast a little**, but do not make it sound too good to be true.

DON'T:
Similar to the approach to keywords and essential criteria, do not copy-paste whatever the job ad states. You do not want to appear too good to be true. Do not overdo it and use many super positive adjectives and

adverbs, such as superb, fantastic, great, huge, enormous, amazing, etc.

DO:

Be honest with yourself and who you are. If your attention to detail is OK, do not say it is "amazing." If your computer skills are average, do not say they are "great," and so on.

WHY: We all smarten up our CVs; that is normal. But when you go overboard, you risk putting yourself in an awkward position, not only at the interview stage but also if you manage to get the job. Imagine you write you are a superb Java developer when in reality, you just finished the course and had two projects. You might be able to fake it at the interview, but once you get the job, it will most definitely show.

3.2. DOCUMENT DESIGN AND LAYOUT

Now that you understand the basics of CV writing, we're moving on to the actual document design and layout.

This is probably the most frequent topic I go over with my clients.

The reason for that is quite simple – over the past few years, there has been a shift in representing yourself to a potential employer. Colorful templates emerged, together with countless CV maker apps, and it is easy to get lost in the colors, shapes, fonts, and icons.

And let's be fair – after long and boring lists, this came as a refreshment.

But the thing is this: recruiters are flooded by these types of CVs. So, **you are no longer an exception.** No one will notice you if you are using the same template other 50 candidates are also using.

Here is what a person who goes through tens, if not hundreds of CVs daily, needs to see: a clear, neat, and organized document that is easy to read.

What do I mean by that?

Firstly, I mean that you need to **write your content horizontally.**

We are most used to presenting things horizontally in

a written form, as opposed to vertically. One of the worst things you can do is to mix horizontal and vertical arrangements.

The reason is that it is challenging to follow, and the reader does not know where they should be looking at first.

Should they focus on the vertical information you provided? Usually, that is the contact details and skills.

Should they focus on the horizontal information first?

Probably **yes** because the information they *are* interested in is there. But *how* are the readers supposed to do that when their eyes automatically go to the margins? There is something in the form of a column, and usually, it is colored, which makes it even more distracting.

See, that is why **the best thing to do is stick to the good, old horizontal representation of information.** It is simple, straightforward, and easy to follow.

Remember, you only have a *few* seconds to grab the reader's attention. You do not want them to waste those precious moments trying to figure out how to read your CV.

Once your CV is fully horizontal, there's a better chance someone will read it.

***

The next thing is also very important, and you need to take it seriously – **do not use** any photographs, icons, diagrams, tables, unusual fonts, timelines, flashy colors, flowers, waves, etc. These things can usually be found in CV templates, and you need to understand that those elements are **distractors.**

Your CV should be professional-looking, and the goal here is to convince the reader you can do the job, not prove you can insert objects in a word processor or modify an online template.

***

Another big thing about the layout and organization of your document is definitely **consistency when presenting something.** This mainly applies to your work experience section.

First, present your work experience in **bullet points** because paragraphs are unsystematic and hard to digest. Then, determine the number of bullet points and make sure to use the **same number** of them throughout the section.

What does this mean in real life? It means that all your positions within the same section need to be presented in the same way. Do not present the first work experience with 4 bullet points, the next one with 9, and then the third one with 2 paragraphs.

Not only does it look untidy, but it is difficult to follow and shows you lack focus and attention to detail.

If you are wondering how is it possible that a reader learns all this based on a simple CV, I will explain it in a few points:

- Untidiness is a pure visual user experience, and surely anyone who opens your CV will notice it.
- If you describe your *second* work experience in the same section differently than you described the first one, it doesn't look good. It seems as if you lack focus. Basically, it's like you forgot how you chose to present your first work experience by the time you got to the second one.
- If you, as a potential employee, use different formatting in a very short document, what can an employer expect to see on the job? They might need you to collect some data, organize it, present it, compile reports, etc. And who would trust you to do these tasks if your CV is messy?
- Related to that is the attention to detail because *obviously,* the person writing the CV (you) completely missed the fact they used different formatting for each work experience they described within the same section.

When we put things in perspective like that, it does not look too promising, does it?

***

When we talk about the **font size** and **style**, I always recommend going with what is considered standard. Avoid unusual fonts that make your CV hard to read and choose any size from 10 to 12 points for the content. The contact information can be 14 points but don't go overboard with that either – you might come off as a narcissist if you use size 20 for your name.

If your CV is content-heavy, it is a good idea to use a smaller font so everything fits on two pages. Readers can zoom in if needed, and the fact your CV is not long is way more important than the font size you use.

Also, if you see that one or two words spill over in the next row or to the next page, try rephrasing your content. There's always another way to say things.

***

Remember to always **capitalize job titles** and **use all caps in moderation.** My recommendation would be to use all caps for section titles and maybe even other elements, like education level or the job title. Whichever option you choose, remember to do it **consistently.** Do not write one section title in all caps and the next one differently. The same goes for any other element you want to write in all caps – check and see if you have done it consistently.

***

Proper alignment is also needed throughout the document. The cleanest look is to align your **section titles center** and your **content left**.

You can also choose to align everything to the left – the important thing is to do it consistently. That way, your reader doesn't have to search for information – you've presented everything clearly, and they know exactly where to look.

***

Here's a quick cheat sheet for you to use, and which summarizes what I've talked about in this part of the Guide:

- Write your CV horizontally. Do not mix vertical data representation, infographics, or tables with the horizontal representation of your data. Those CVs tend to be confusing as the reader doesn't know where to look first.
- To separate your sections and to provide a better visual experience, you can use border lines between them (type ---, ***, or ### and press enter, for example).
- Rephrase your bullet point/CV content if you see that one word spills over to the next row or page. That way, you save valuable page space.
- Make sure your document's orientation is "Portrait."

- Consistency is important. Triple-check your CV for consistency: font, alignment, and the number of bullet points.
- Do not use unusual-looking fonts because you think it's *cool*. It might be cool to you because you're only reading the one CV you wrote, but to a person who has to read 50 others, it is distracting and often unappealing.
- Do not use flashy colors, photos, timelines, or icons. The reason is the same as the one mentioned above.
- Do not put information in the header/footer. It makes CVs look untidy. Not only that, but you will be repeating information on every page of your document.

What we covered in this part of the Guide applies to **most** professions and, therefore, most CVs. Of course, there are exceptions if you need to display your creativity, but this Guide is to help the majority, so my focus is to teach the majority how to write a smashing CV. And a smashing CV can transform your career and your life.

3.3. WRITING CV SECTIONS

You now understand how your CV should look and sound like. We will move on to writing sections that every single CV needs to have.

3.3.1. BASIC INFORMATION

Before you get to anything else, you need to share your contact information. Make sure to use your **current mobile phone number** and an **email address you frequently check.**

There is no need to write your home address, as this is something that has been done in the past when people were actually sending their job applications by post.

As mentioned above, your whole CV should be horizontal and your contact info should be presented in two lines, right below your name. There is no need to introduce a column to share your contact information.

3.3.2. WRITING A PERSONALIZED AND HUMAN-FRIENDLY CV

The word "personalized" is an adjective, and it means "designed or produced to meet someone's individual requirements."

I would like to emphasize that last part, so you really understand it – *someone's individual requirements*. In this case, that someone is **you.**

That is why **I do not use templates, and that is why you're not going to use one either.** Why? Templates do not do you justice! You are an individual with your own background, personality, and experience.

Even if two people wanted a CV for exactly the same position, I assure you their **CVs would not be the same.** Of course, some touchpoints would exist because their CVs would be focused on the same position, but **each CV is personalized to fit who they are.** There is no template for that.

Their CVs simply cannot be the same! Their experience varies; their skills are different, as well as their personalities.

I would not want to get someone in trouble by saying they are focused on details if they had a lot of typos in their original CV, for example. Not even if attention to detail is a job requirement. And that's the principle you need to follow, too. You might have some really great skills that fit the job requirement, but if you don't have a specific skill or a personality trait, just skip it. You have plenty to offer, so one little thing will not hold you back!

***

If you're not new to job search, you probably heard about ATS or software that scans candidates' CVs and organizes them into a "yes" and "no" pile. While that is true, and some companies really do use software for that initial screening, you need to know that you can't write a CV for the software alone.

Your CV has to be human-friendly.

Software can't pick up the phone and give you a call to discuss your suitability for the role. An actual person has to do that, and before they do, they need to look at your CV.

If your CV is not satisfactory, if it takes too long to understand your background, or if it is just plain confusing, you **will not get that call.**

Besides, we all know computers can have software bugs. Someone needs to double-check their work. And who does it? A human being – that's right. So, while you need to have in mind the fact that your CV will be scanned, you also need to have in mind the fact that you'll have to impress a real person as well.

***

What I am trying to tell you is that **you only have a few seconds to get someone's attention.** Just like you have a few seconds to leave a good first impression.

Now, if you only have a few seconds, you better write something impressive and worth reading! Instead of using online templates, corny phrases, and keywords that **do not apply** to your professional life situation, you need to completely personalize your CV!

3.3.3. FLEXIBILITY OF THE CV STRUCTURE

Following the logic that your CV needs to be personalized, we can conclude that your CV structure and content, therefore, are entirely dependent on who **you** are.

Because of that, you need to create a CV that makes you look like the best candidate for your desired job. Since the foundation of the job application and relevant background is different for everyone, you need to know that the structure of a CV is not set in stone.

I have noticed what brings the best results to my clients. That is giving the reader a **quick overview of why you're the best person for the job.** Basically, you need to write a brief and tidy overview in several bullet points as your first section. In those bullet points, list what makes you the perfect candidate for the job.

Think of this as your "best-of," something that must be known about you as a professional. In your opening section (opener), **combine** educational background, relevant experience, and skills/personality traits, whichever is most relatable.

In this section, incorporate keywords you find in the job ad(s), as well as job requirements and "nice-to-haves."

As mentioned earlier, be mindful of **how** you incorporate those keywords. Everything has to read fluently, it shouldn't be too obvious, and you need to include only those things that actually make sense when looking at your background.

***

Now, let's look into what it means that your CV's structure is flexible.

You can have your opening section and then go straight into your work experience. Or maybe your education is super relevant – in that case, you will not forcingly write about your work experience just because you've seen templates where work experience *always* comes after the opening section.

You need to write a CV that you're comfortable with and which reflects who you are.

Because the structure of a CV is flexible, you can move the sections around! That gives you the freedom to personalize your CV completely.

Instead of sticking to some template you found online which outlines an imaginary "perfect" CV structure, you do whatever works for you.

Also, do not copy your friend's or colleague's CV – you are not taking a test.

4. THE OPENING SECTION OF YOUR CV

Let's dig a bit deeper into this opening section business.

If you have ever tried to write a CV and you used a CV template, you probably noticed they have one thing in common – an opening section that provides some sort of an overview. Even the templates got this right, so you can imagine how important it is.

Here are some title suggestions for this section:

- (Career) Objective
- Personal Statement
- Executive Summary
- Professional Summary
- Professional Profile

The idea of opening a CV with an overview section is absolutely fantastic! But it needs to be done right, and it most definitely can not look like a cover letter. So, forget about paragraphs and mini-essays. You need to use concise bullet points that convince the reader you're the perfect person for the job.

I am sure you have heard that a recruiter or a hiring manager spends only a **few seconds** looking at your CV. That is because they have a bunch of them sitting in their inbox, and they have to use their time wisely.

To be efficient and effective, they simply skim the CVs. You need something to grab their attention, and it has to be **presented to them at the very beginning.** A good approach is to think of your opening section as a great and exciting movie trailer that makes you want to see the entire movie.

This is actually your "hook," which will ensure someone reads your whole CV. That is why this section has to be your "best-of." If you fail to entice the reader in this first section, they will not read your CV.

***

Since it is not easy to skim through paragraphs, your "best-of" has to be presented in **understandable and clear bullet points relevant to the job ad.**

What do I mean by "relevant"?

Relevant is whatever makes you seem like a great candidate for the position you are applying to. Remember, here, we're building a case. We're explaining why **you** are the best person for the job.

Therefore, the key is to focus precisely on those things that emphasize you are a good match. I would recommend using 5 to 10 bullet points here, depending on your situation.

This has been the staple of my success in CV writing, and therefore my clients' success. For this reason, I am sure that if you follow the steps outlined in this Guide, you will gain traction with your CV, too!

***

So, your aim in the introductory section of a CV is to write a good "hook." Something that will make the reader want to find out more about you.

Your first section needs to be a combination of the lists I asked you to compile. Take a close look at those and see what your "best of" is for the job position you want. This opening section should be a killer combo of your skills, traits, and certificates. Something that a recruiter/hiring manager can't say "no" to.

To put it simply: **give the reader what they want** – a candidate who is qualified for the role. Use the keywords and use them so it's not too obvious you're shoving them down their throat. :)

***

The next thing I'd like to cover is choosing the **title of the opening section.**

No matter what title you choose, you have to be aware of one thing: **your section title has to be aligned with what you are presenting in the section.**

Meaning, if you do not have the actual education, confirmations of course attendance, or certificates, do not use the word "qualification." You can be deeply knowledgeable about a specific subject, but if you do not have a **paper to prove it**, steer clear of any words that might suggest otherwise.

Similarly, if you decide to use the phrase "relevant skills" in your title section, you need to be mindful of what you present in it. Do not list skills that are **not** relevant to the job. No one has time for those, *especially* after you said you would only list the relevant ones. Do your research and make sure each and every skill (or ability) you mention in this section is indeed **relevant** to the position you are applying to.

And just so we're on the same page, I want to be extra clear about this and explain *why* the section title is important. With it, you set **expectations** for your reader.

It is like a promise you give your readers, and if they do not find what they were expecting, they will be disappointed.

Some can even stop reading your CV because you failed to deliver.

Just think about how you felt the last time you clicked on an article because of its brilliant headline, only to realize it was clickbait.

If the headline is misleading, do you feel like reading the article all the way through? Probably not.

In the same way, you do not want the person reading your CV to stop just because you mistitled your opening section.

As they say, the devil is in the details, so keep an eye out on every little thing.

4.1. TONE AND STYLE OF THE OPENING SECTION

And lastly, let's go over the requirements for the tone and style of the opening section.

You already know a lot about this, so a quick cheat sheet for you to follow will suffice:

- Your tone and style need to be objective and professional
- Use bullet points because they give a clearer overview of your "best of"
- Discretely incorporate relatable keywords
- Use verbs instead of nouns
- Avoid overexplaining and too many details
- Don't use personal pronouns as it's not professional

5. SPECIFIC CV SECTIONS

Once you have your opening section ready, it is time to move on to the next one.

Your information should be presented in **order of importance** because you have very limited time to grab the reader's attention.

To put it simply, **think of your CV as an inverted pyramid.**

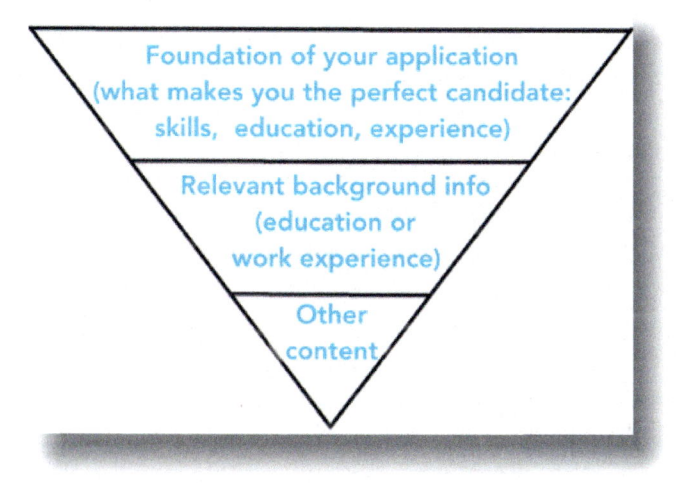

Foundation of your application
(what makes you the perfect candidate: skills, education, experience)

Relevant background info
(education or work experience)

Other content

Your basis is the first section, the opener. This is the foundation of your application.

What you write next is also important, and most people *will* stick around to read it because it is on the first page. It is right there in front of them, so they will most likely read it.

However, keep in mind that with each section you add, the **importance lowers**. Whatever information is in the **first half of the first page** needs to be relevant and intriguing enough for the reader to continue.

The importance of your content should lower as the reader scans your CV from top to bottom. That is because your reader is losing focus with each passing second. You should not take it personally; it is just something that happens to humans – we lose focus.

So, because of this simple fact, you need to **start with the essential information**. Start with something that everyone in the professional world needs to know about you. Then, continue with something less important. Remember to **leave out** any information that is **not relevant** to the job position or the field you are applying to. It only creates clutter, and it does not add value to your CV.

***

There are two ways about the second section – you either have **valuable, relevant work experience** or a **strong, relevant educational background**.

If you happen to have both, I always recommend **starting with the real-life experience**.

That does not mean that your education is not important; it just means that I personally believe nothing trumps experience. You are actually utilizing knowledge acquired through education and applying it in real life, which is way more relevant than just learning the theory of doing things.

With this in mind, look at your lists again. Then, look at the role or the field for which you are writing the CV.

What would make a more powerful statement?

How should you present yourself?

What would say "this person is perfect for the job" to the reader?

***

Now that you have thought about it and decided on the way to go, it is time you roll up your sleeves and get to writing.

Here is a reminder of what your dedicated sections should have – a **purpose.**

The purpose of your CV is to land you a job interview.

And this means that **every single line has to bring value to the reader** and present you in a positive way.

If something does not bring value, it only creates clutter.

5.1. PRESENTING YOUR WORK EXPERIENCE

When applying for a job, you can have **three types of work experience.** This is based on how high the correlation is between the positions you had and the one you want now.

You can either have relevant, related, or unrelated work experience.

Each of those is different, so you have to present each of them differently in your CV.

You can't describe a past (or current) position that **entirely corresponds** to the position you want now *in the same way* as you would describe a position that is **unrelated** to what you want to do now.

It will not help your goal of getting a job interview, and you will most likely confuse the reader. They will expect everything you presented to be equally important. And you want to be very clear and specific when giving information. You can't expect your reader to know what's the most important part of your work history – you have to spell it out for them. I like to say that we need to spoon-feed the reader relevant information.

In reality, this means that:

- You will not dedicate a lot of space in your CV to the positions that are **not relevant** to the field you are interested in. For example, there is no reason to describe a waitressing position in detail if you are now applying for a job in graphic design.

- You will not describe in detail a position that you held 20 years ago and which lasted only a few weeks. Even if it *is* relevant, times change, and the way we did things 20 years ago in any branch differs from how we are doing things now.

Remember, **page space is precious**, and you do not want to waste it on anything that does not bring you closer to your goal.

And your goal is to get to the job interview phase.

In order to do that, you need to convince the reader you are the perfect person for the job.

***

Some jobseekers have only one type of work experience while others might have all three. It doesn't really matter in which group you fall into. However, what does matter is *how* you present your work experience. You have to have **separate sections for different types of work experience** in your CV.

5.1.1. TONE, STYLE, AND KEYWORDS IN WORK EXPERIENCE DESCRIPTIONS

Before we dive into specific types of work experience, I will go over some do's and don'ts when it comes to the tone and style of writing and the use of keywords.

As previously stated, your CV should reflect who you are as a professional.

Therefore, your tone needs to be **professional** and **objective** in the work experience sections, too.

Same as in the opening section, steer clear of any slang, idioms, and other terms which may be deemed as "unprofessional."

Remember the goal of your CV and tailor all content to fit it.

DON'T:

In this role, I was in charge of supervising the production.
My job was to collect data and enter it into a computer.
I handled cybersecurity, investigated weird actions, and flagged misfits in the community.

DO:

- Scheduled and managed the production process
- Collected, analyzed, sorted, and entered data into a system application

- Maintained safe cyberspace, investigated activities, and flagged suspicious accounts and users

WHY: Steer clear from personal pronouns and sentences. Avoid full sentences because bullet points are easier to read and follow in a CV. Do not use inappropriate language which reflects your own opinion of the job. Keep it clean and professional.

***

When we talk about presenting work experience, remember we're actually talking about **describing your past (and current) positions.**

Because these are precise portrayals of your roles, in these sections, it is OK to use **more field-related acronyms and terms.**

Still, I would encourage you to use clear language that everyone can understand, but this truly depends on the profession.

And when I say to use clear language, I mean **calling it what it is.**

If you worked as a waiter and had to take orders and clear tables, say it just the way it is. You can spruce it up a bit and go fancy, but do not make it sound like you were defusing bombs.

DON'T:
> I showed knowledge of GMP, SOP, HACCP, and safety regulations.
>
> Worked in many programming languages and familiar with object-oriented programming techniques.
>
> I attended to the needs of bar guests, presented the drinks selection, followed secret house recipes, and prepared outstanding alcoholic mixes to quench their thirst.

DO:
- Adhered to standard operating procedures, good manufacturing practice, HACCP principles, and safety regulations
- Worked in HTML, CSS, XML, PHP and familiar with object-oriented programming techniques
- Greeted and seated guests, presented the menu, prepared, and served cocktails

WHY: Some things are considered common knowledge, like, for example, HACCP. While SOP and GMP make perfect sense to you, sometimes we need to spell it out for others. As I said earlier, some acronyms you can't avoid.

Don't be shy and not list something just because it is an acronym, and you feel like it would be bragging.

When it comes to business-specific software, of course, you have to list them, especially if they are well-known.

Balance is key, and the point is to have an **understandable CV** that will bring the desired results. Also, a quick reminder that it needs to be understandable to others, not just to you.

***

Another point that deserves attention in this section of the Guide is **keywords**! Descriptions of your past positions are perfect spots for introducing keywords. So is your current position, just so we're clear.

What you need to do is this:
- **Scan quite a few job ads** for the position you are applying to. Even if you have the link to the exact position you want, check out a few others as well. I would recommend 5 at least.
- Similarly, **check at least 5 job descriptions** for your desired position. Literally, do a web search with your job title + "job description" and check out various sites. Looking at other job descriptions can help your CV writing immensely.
- **Compile a list of keywords and phrases** you often see in the job description and requirements sections. There are some things that are repeated in the content you've found when you carried out the search. Of course, choose only words and

phrases which apply to your past positions so you can link the two and present them as a meaningful whole.
- **Utilize those keywords** in your CV by incorporating them into the job descriptions.

Whatever you do, **do not take the keywords and introduce them in a separate section.**

As I said in the previous chapter, those keywords have to read fluently and fit the context. That is the only appropriate way to do it.

You could put two similar keywords together or combine them with your own material. In fact, that would be desirable, so it's less obvious what you've done.

DON'T:
- Copy-paste entire sections that refer to the job description and job requirements:
    - Provide Secretarial Support to the Partner and Team
    - Audio typing
    - Prepare and processing documents
    - Drafting and amending court documents, letters, and other documentation accurately

- Communicating with and assisting clients and staff
- General reception duties

DO:
- Read the job ads carefully and see how you can utilize those keywords that keep reappearing in different advertisements:
    - Drafted, typed, amended, and processed documents in a timely manner
    - Handled general administrative duties and provided secretarial support to the management
    - Communicated with the clients and staff in person, over the phone, and email

WHY: Combining various keywords makes your CV more concise because you use one bullet point instead of two. Also, you're getting the same point across. This is always a plus when you have limited page space. And by adding your own few words, you are making sure it is not too obvious you copy-pasted the job ad.

***

And there is one final thing I'd like to bring to your attention when it comes to presenting work experience – **tenses**.

I see this mistake time after time again in my clients' submitted CVs. Native English speakers make it just as often as non-native speakers do. The only logical explanation is that they are not paying attention.

If you are describing a **past** work experience, you need to refer to it in the **past tense.** It is as simple as that!

Likewise, if you are describing a current position, you need to use present continuous so it is correctly presented.

5.1.2. PRESENTING RELEVANT WORK EXPERIENCE

If you have all three types of work experience, there is **no need to list them all**. Depending on how extensive your experience is, you can opt for **relevant experience only.**

That way, you will keep your CV nice, clean, and presentable. There is no need to add other types of work experiences unless you feel like the actual relevant experience is **not rich enough.**

Also, remember to title your section accordingly and try to keep it simple. "Relevant Work Experience" is a great choice.

***

Your experience is relevant if you carried out at least **some of the duties** mentioned in the job ad. Now, the only thing you need to do is present those duties in a transparent and straightforward way, so everyone sees just **how relevant** your experience is. The best way to show off your relevant experience is to do detailed research and incorporate keywords in your job duties descriptions, just like we talked about earlier. Also, remember to do that with bullet points.

If the role is/was complex or a bit general, it would be beneficial to add a few **introductory sentences** that explain the main objective of the role.

The idea of those introductory sentences is to help the reader understand your role better. As you probably know, there are numerous job titles that cover the same or similar duties. Due to that, the reader does not know if your **particular job title matches what they need.** To make sure they understand you indeed *are* the perfect person for the role, you need to explain the nature of your job in a few introductory sentences.

***

Think about it this way: if you have never heard of this job title, what would help you understand it?

You can cover some general duties you had, what you have learned, or what kind of skills you have developed during your employment. Whatever you deem important enough when you talk about the role but *not* specific duties, as those need to go in the bullet points.

Some good examples of introductory sentences are:

- "Worked as a part of a production team carrying out welding, grinding, and painting duties. Learned how to operate various hand and power tools while adhering to company procedures."

- "Worked at the accounts department at the company that represents import, distribution, and trade partners in the market. Demonstrated excellent attention to detail and the ability to organize workload and complete tasks on time."

- "Successfully fulfilled administrative duties and assisted the company's employees in the office and court. Gained experience in legal proceedings and documentation and showed great dedication, adaptability, and ability to learn and improve quickly."

5.1.3. PRESENTING RELATED WORK EXPERIENCE

If you do not have the actual *relevant experience* but have experience working in roles that are *kind of similar* or can be *associated* in any way with what you want to do next, you have what I refer to as **related experience.**

By using this phrase, you are honest in saying your experience is **not** relevant, but it is intriguing enough for the reader to read the section.

Here, I would also suggest keeping it simple and titling the section describing this type of experience "Related Work Experience."

***

A great example would be using your experience as a Retail Store Assistant when you want to switch to any other customer-focused role, like in a call center or a restaurant.

What makes it "related" is the nature of the job – you worked in a team in a busy environment, communicated with customers, advised on product selection, handled complaints, were required to be calm and professional, etc.

When it comes to the job descriptions themselves, make sure to **emphasize the parts that correlate** with what you want to do next.

For example, if you had worked in retail and want to switch to an office environment, your job descriptions would need to look like this:

- Handled delivery related documentation and utilized office equipment
- Assisted customers in locating needed items
- Kept the store organized, clean, and presentable at all times

This way, you show that you are organized, familiar with computer work, and used to handling customer queries. These skills are also desirable in an office environment, so you need to emphasize them.

Basically, what you need to do is **find a connection between your work experience and your desired position.** Use the job ad(s) and job descriptions to find keywords and see how you can incorporate them in your related work experience section.

***

When we're talking about presenting work experience, your relevant experience should always be presented first (of course, if you have it). Then, if you feel like your relevant experience is not rich enough, add a section outlining your related experience.

That way, you can enrich your CV and paint a better picture while staying on a topic that interests your reader.

Enriching is great, but if you choose to do this, be mindful you don't overdo it – your CV still needs to be clear, tailored for a specific job ad, and tidy.

Remember **not to go over two pages.** It is *extremely* rare that someone needs more than two pages, even if they have a lot of experience.

There is always a way to present yourself more effectively.

5.1.4. PRESENTING UNRELATED WORK EXPERIENCE

I am sure many will benefit from the above advice, but what happens if you have no relevant nor related experience?

What if you are changing careers and only have *unrelated* work experience?

Well, what you want to do in those cases is go with a simple "Work History" or "Work Experience" section. If you have a rich work background, you can even use "Highlighted Work Experience," so it is clear what you listed is just **a selection** of your work history that you decided to present. Remember, you need to write your CV on one page (ideally) or two pages (acceptable), which is why having a *selection* of your work experience is an excellent idea.

***

Whichever title you go with, try to **keep the job descriptions simple** because they are not exactly relevant nor related to what you are looking to do next.

Of course, you want to present your duties, but there is **no reason** why you should have more than three bullet points.

The only exception would be if this unrelated position was/is your **only work experience.** Then, it is OK to have five or six bullet points, but do not go into details of your role because the reader will most probably not be interested. After all, it does not correlate at all with the job you are applying to now.

Here are a few bullet points to show you how it is supposed to look in real life:

- Participated in developing sales strategies to draw in potential buyers
- Collected, analyzed, and presented performance data
- Cleaned and maintained communal areas and houses to ensure dignified living conditions

See, with this, you briefly explain your role, but you do not bore the reader. Your job descriptions are accurate and elegant, and if the reader wants to know more about a particular topic, they will ask you at the job interview.

***

So, to conclude, **it is not the end of the world if you do not have relevant or related experience.** You just need to find your angle and focus on facts that *do* make you a good candidate.

These can be **soft skills** that are important for the role, like people skills, social skills, communication skills, personality traits, adaptability, work ethic, problem-solving skills, etc. Or it can be your **educational**

background that is important for the role, and that will help you get the job interview invitation.

You need to have a foundation and a reason as to *why* you are switching careers. Usually, it is a completed course or a degree. Of course, in theory, you can just wake up one day and decide to become a graphic designer and start doing it. But remember, a certificate goes a long way! You can definitely focus your CV on a certificate and use it to show why you *are* the perfect candidate.

***

Remember, **the structure of your CV is flexible.** If the only work experience you have is unrelated and you have completed a course, you will not present your experience before education. Refer to the inverted pyramid for a reminder of how to structure your CV. :)

5.2. PRESENTING YOUR EDUCATIONAL BACKGROUND, COURSES, AND TRAINING

First, refer to the list of completed programs I asked you to compile. Chances are, there will be some things that do not correlate with what you want to do now. You can leave those out, just like you have left out other irrelevant information.

Once you have done that, let's look into the ways of presenting your educational background. The way is, of course, closely connected to the goal of your CV. That means it will depend on your situation and the purpose of this section.
Always keep in mind what you are trying to achieve with your CV. It needs to reflect what you want to do next and show the reader how exactly you fit the role. If your educational background clearly indicates why you're qualified for the job, make sure to emphasize it. You need to apply the same logic to this section as to any other.

The title of the section needs to reflect what's presented in it. I would recommend keeping it simple – go with something like **"Education & Training"** or **"Professional Training & Certificates."**

***

Here is what you *need* to outline in this section, regardless of how much emphasis you put on it:

- Name of the institution that issued the certificate/diploma
- Location of the institution
- Program title
- Year (month) of issuance and expiry (if applicable)

***

In this section, you can describe **any** professional training, course, workshop, research, webinar, and even conference you attended. If something has enriched you as a professional and is relevant to what you want to do now, you can mention it here.

And that includes **online learning platforms and online universities.** I want to talk about those specifically because often, people think they "don't count."

This misconception is not uncommon because online learning was seen as less valuable or even completely fake and made fun of just a few years ago.

Thankfully, more and more people are beginning to see that the *traditional* formal education does not follow the needs of our world. Education systems across the globe are outdated because they are based on memorizing information that today we have at our fingertips. That is precisely why online learning is booming, and our society is starting to look at it differently.

Still, despite the progress we've made, you need to be careful about **which online learning platforms you present in your CV.** Some of them do have a bad reputation.

The best thing to do is check out the institution before starting the program, but if you haven't done so, please do it before you add it to your CV.

***

This section is also an excellent opportunity to mention any type of education that was organized by a company you worked for. This includes **in-house training sessions, courses, and workshops.**

Of course, some companies make it clear that those certificates are valid while you are with them. What this means in real life is that those are useless elsewhere because they were internal programs.

However, **if you are struggling with the educational background section**, a great way to fill it would be to list the in-house training you completed. It does not have to be very detailed, but it **can** be in your CV.

***

And one last thing before we dive into describing your educational background - you can, and you should also **add ongoing programs to your CV.** This shows a willingness to learn and your determination to get better in a specific field so it can't hurt to have it in your CV.

5.2.1. PRESENTING EDUCATIONAL BACKGROUND, COURSES, AND TRAINING WHEN SWITCHING CAREERS

If you are switching careers and have completed suitable courses you need to kick-start it, I would, without doubt, suggest you **make your CV all about the newly acquired qualifications.**

Here is how you should do it:

- **Describe the program(s) in a few sentences.** Briefly explain what you have learned, what you are qualified to do, and mention practical coursework. Basically, write anything that shows how *amazing* the program was and why you should be hired to do the job. This should be an overview.
- **Describe the curriculum by listing the modules covered.** Having specific names of the modules can help because it gives more insight into what you have learned. It adds clarity to your CV.

***

Let's say your current situation is this: you want to start a career in digital marketing, and you have completed a course to be able to do it.

In your CV, do not simply state you completed "Introduction to Digital Marketing," thinking the reader will know exactly what it covered. **Make some**

effort and present to the reader what you have learned. That way, they will know for sure.

Most program titles are quite generic anyway, and their scope is not always clear. So, you need to **specify** and make sure you present what you've learned. That way, whoever reads your CV will know exactly what you're qualified to do.

A few examples of describing newly acquired qualifications/educational background when you don't have relevant work experience would be:
"Learned how to identify and address core issues in public governance while considering the challenges raised by global processes. Also learned about the public policy changes in various administrative areas. Gained in-depth knowledge of classifying risk management situations, collecting and analyzing data, collaborating on alternative methods of resolution, and assessing results. Became familiar with the nature and formation of various businesses as well as government law that is applied to public and non-profit administration leadership and policy. Courses covered the areas of public speaking, grant writing, database management, accounting, statistics, and law throughout this versatile degree."

"Currently attending the graduate program in HR Management and learning about current issues in the

HR Management domain, how to develop and implement strategies for improvement, which will benefit all levels of employees.

Courses covered: *International Corporate Strategy, Professional Employment Law, HRM in Context, Applied Corporate Strategy, Employee Engagement, Leading, Managing & Developing, Training & Knowledge Management, Research Methods, Reward & Incentive Management, Performance Management, Sourcing & Testing. The program also included workshops in Coaching and Mentoring.*

Acquired an understanding of the role of human resources in modern organizations, from hiring procedures to strategies for motivating employees, and systems for developing and retaining talent."

"Completed a course which incorporated finance, valuation, financial modeling, budgeting and forecasting, accounting, and strategy topics. Learned how to use advanced Excel functions and formulas (XNPV, XIRR, PMT, IPMT, VLOOKUP, CHOOSE, INDEX MATCH MATCH, OFFSET), budgeting tools, and financial dashboards. Modules included: *Financial Analysis Fundamentals, Financial Modelling with VBA, Budgeting and Forecasting, Scenario and Data Visualisation, Behavioural Finance Fundamentals, Building a Financial Model in Excel, Business Valuation Modelling, FP&A Monthly Cash Flow Forecasting, M&A Modelling.*"

This approach applies even when you have **related experience** because you are sort of switching careers in that scenario, too. You need to have a reason why you want to move from one *kind of similar* position to another. And this section is precisely the time and place where you explain it.

It might seem like a massive chunk of text, and I've told you to avoid paragraphs, but in this case, it's a necessity. You need to explain what you've learned and why you're the perfect person for the job despite not having super relevant work experience. And you simply can't do that if you don't deep-dive into your education.

When writing about your education, be precise and clear – each sentence needs to add value to the CV. Don't just throw in sentences there; ask yourself: "Why is this important?" and "What do I want to achieve with this particular sentence?".

***

You can also present your educational background in detail if you are very proud of it and you have limited relevant work experience. Don't forget you can also move CV sections around and see what works best!

5.2.2. PRESENTING EDUCATIONAL BACKGROUND, COURSES, AND TRAINING WHEN YOU HAVE RELEVANT WORK EXPERIENCE

If you are not switching careers and have **both** relevant work experience and educational background, you have the luxury of choosing **how detailed this section should be.**
There is no pressure of "proving" the reader why you are the right fit because you have the most valuable requirement – relevant work experience.

However, some job ads require certain professional certificates, so make sure not to forget to add them to your CV.

***

Be it as it may, you *need* to dedicate space to education and training. It is crucial to present yourself correctly in a CV. If you have a certificate that is relevant to the field, it should be mentioned, **even if it is not listed as a requirement** in the job ad.
Describe it in a **similar way** as if you were switching careers, only **less detailed.**

One option is listing the main few modules instead of all of them and keeping the overview part to a minimum (one or two sentences).

How will you describe your educational background depends on your situation, so make sure you know **exactly** what you want to achieve when writing about it.

A few examples of presenting educational background when you have relevant experience would be:

"The study program consisted of lectures and practice. Over the 4 years of the program, had student placement in 5 different libraries where learned about the functioning of a library first-hand and developed skills needed to work independently."

"Learned all about modern-day learning techniques and teaching methods and had practical coursework and student placement in a secondary school. Acquired knowledge of didactics, pedagogy, teaching methodology, and was trained on how to track students' performance and provide feedback."

"As a part of in-house training, completed the Care Skills course, which included the following modules: *Parkinson's Disease, Ear Diseases and Deafness, Thyroid Disorder, Alzheimer's Disease, Preventative Healthcare.*"

It is always good to **give an overview of the program**, mention some **modules,** and perhaps **practical skills** developed during the program itself. Keep in mind that the reader doesn't know you, so you have to explain everything to them.

***

If your CV is very rich and you feel like going into any kind of detail would make it too long and hard to digest, **you can always leave out certain information.** Simply say you are fully qualified to work in the field upon completion of the program.

Remember, this is *your* CV, and you need to personalize it to fit *your* situation while clearly showing who you are.

5.2.3. PRESENTING UNRELATED EDUCATIONAL BACKGROUND

Sometimes, people get into a field that has nothing to do with their formal educational background.

In those situations, companies usually organize in-house training sessions. Some even offer to fund a certificate or two, so they are 100% sure their employees are good to go.

If you have an educational background that is entirely unrelated to the field you are interested in, you still need to list it in your CV, just for good measure.

***

Some job ads require you to have a certain level of education, like a secondary school diploma or a bachelor's degree. It does not even have to be a specific degree; you just need to have it.

In those situations, a simple list would do – enough for you to present your background but not too long, so you do not waste precious page space.

It goes without saying that, in these scenarios, this section should always be the last one because it is **irrelevant.**

How you present your educational background in a few words depends on your situation, country of residence, and country of the job poster.

You need to **make sure the reader understands your level of education** if you are applying abroad **or** if you have completed your program abroad. This is very important because if you provide a list with no explanation, the reader has *very* little to go on. Either "translate" your degree or very briefly explain it. That way, the reader will understand what your level of education is.

A few examples of simply listing your educational background would be:
"Completed a secondary vocational school and acquired a secondary school diploma."
"RQF Level 3 General Certificate of Education"
"Completed a 4-year secondary school – equivalent to national level 5 qualification."

6. INCREASE YOUR CHANCES OF SUCCESS

If you followed the CV writing principles laid out in this Guide, then by now, you should have your winning CV written. Congratulations!

Before sending your CV, **do not forget to proofread it.** That way, you will avoid mistakes such as typos or double spaces. Use the default spell checker, but also run it through other tools, such as Grammarly.

6.1. FINE-TUNING YOUR CV

Once that is done, and you are sure your CV is good to go, save it, and make it clear in the file name that it is your **starting point**, your **base.**

I am calling it your base because **you should have several versions of a CV.**

I am sure you have heard this before and let me tell you, it is actually true.

Ideally, you will **adapt your CV to each and every job position you apply to** by introducing keywords from the job ad. We talked about it earlier. This way, you have a better chance of passing the screening software.

These adjustments can be really subtle: instead of using the word "great," you use the word "excellent" because that is how the requirements are listed in the job ad.

Another important thing would be to **follow the patterns** they use and not put together similar phrases if the job ad does not.

For example, you could have 5 years of experience in people and project management, but if the job ad refers to those separately, you should too. Instead of writing "Experienced in people and project management," it is better to say "Experienced in people management" and perhaps in another bullet point, refer to your experience in "project management." This is just to be on the safe side and only if you have enough page space to do it. If at all possible, do not break the phrase, as the software might not catch it.

***

Adapting is an absolute must if you wrote a CV for a field or a profession and not a specific role.

Professions and areas of interest are, in most cases, very broad. Take, for example, cybersecurity or office assistant roles – you can have tens of variations within those fields. For your CV to be effective, you need to

tailor it properly. The only way you can optimize your CV is by focusing it on a **single** position.

***

If you do not want to amend your CV for every single job ad (role, position), then at least **group** them. The more you narrow the focus of your CV, the better chances you have of success because you will be able to optimize the CV better. So, instead of having quite a generic CV that covers a whole field, **adjust your CV to more specific areas of interest.**

In the two examples I mentioned earlier, some of the groups would be:

- For cybersecurity: cyber forensics, penetration tester, risk management
- For office positions: reception, accounting assistant, office management

You might be the perfect candidate, but if your CV does not show it, no one will recognize it, and then it won't really matter.

So, in order for your CV to bring results, remember that **the most important thing is to tailor it.**

6.2. THINK ABOUT SOCIAL MEDIA

Since we live in a digital world and social media platforms are just a click away, you also need to think of your representation there. Together with fine-tuning your CV, this step is also important for increasing your chances of success.

Make sure to align your CV with what you have stated on various profiles, especially LinkedIn if you are on it (and you should definitely be, as it can boost your job search immensely).

No matter how many different versions of a CV you write, you need to keep in mind that anyone can look you up. It is very simple, and recruiters do it. Curiosity is natural, and you do not want to have huge discrepancies between your CV and what you stated on LinkedIn, for example.

Some discrepancies are acceptable, and with CV section titles, you can cover yourself nicely. That is why titling is super important. However, you still need to have an explanation for whatever discrepancy there is. It might come up at a job interview, and you do not want to be surprised by it.

For example, if you have chosen to leave out some roles from your CV because you do not feel comfortable discussing them, definitely remove them from LinkedIn and other platforms. That way, no one will be able to ask you questions about it. On the other hand, if you have left out a role because it is not relevant to the job you are interested in now, you do not have to remove it from LinkedIn. There is no real harm in that, and you can simply say it is not in your CV because it is not relevant to the field.

As with everything in CV writing, this also depends on **your** situation.

7. THE IMPORTANCE OF COVER LETTERS

You are all ready for **CV writing** *Linking Lines style*, but before you start your next job search, I would like to bring your attention to the importance of cover letters.

Often, the **cover letter is the initial contact between a job applicant and the job poster.** That is why it needs to be of high quality. **Imagine no one even gets to your CV because of a poorly written cover letter!** Then all your hard work would be in vain. To ensure this does not happen, you need to pay attention to your cover letter.

***

Many are confused with the concept of cover letters, and I often get queries about them. I will list the most common ones and answer them straight away, so we settle the question of cover letters once and for all.

- **What is a cover letter?**

A cover letter is actually quite similar to a motivational letter, but it also has the purpose of explaining why it is that **you** should get the job.

So, your cover letter needs to tell the reader the following:

- what is your motivation for the role – why are you applying for *that* particular role at *that* particular company
- what can you bring to the table – why are you a good fit, why should they hire *you*, how will they benefit from it
- why are you looking for a job – explain what is going on in your career and why is it that you are looking for a job *at this moment*

- **Should I write a cover letter when applying for a job?**

Yes, you should. In my opinion, that is how you show you are genuinely interested in the position and the company.

Many candidates are in a time crunch, and if they see the cover letter is optional, they will not send it in.

Don't you think it looks better for you as a professional if you always write a few words expressing your interest?

- **Do people even read cover letters?**

Yes, they do. Especially if the job applications are submitted via email and not through a company recruitment software. In those cases, your email *is* the cover letter, and it is always better to have a proper cover letter than to write a short email saying, "Here is my CV attached."

Besides, even if no one reads the cover letter, it's better to be safe than sorry, right?

7.1. TONE, STYLE, AND KEYWORDS IN A COVER LETTER

Your CV gives insight into who you are as a professional, and your tone needs to be professional and objective.

Cover letters are slightly different.

Cover letters are where you can throw in a bit of personality. If you have a hobby that can be related to the role or the field, you can mention it in your cover letter.

***

You have to use personal pronouns in cover letters, and your tone can be a bit less formal. After all, you *are* writing a letter.

That being said, it does not mean you can use slang or any business-inappropriate language. Your cover letter is still a representation of who you are as a professional, even if you can mention your hobby in it.

***

Here comes the super important bit: **keywords should also be incorporated in your cover letter.**

The process is the same as for your CV – do your research and add phrases to your cover letter. Remember to use only those keywords that apply to you and include them in your content so they read fluently.

***

And just one final reminder – **always proofread your cover letters!**

7.2. THE STRUCTURE OF A COVER LETTER

Now that we have cleared the air regarding the style, tone, and keywords, let's look into the structure and layout of your cover letter.

Just like CVs, cover letters also need to be **understandable to others.** Keep this in mind when writing one. Cover letters need to be organized in appropriate paragraphs and make a meaningful whole.

A cover letter needs to give a brief overview of your background and skills (a few sentences). When I say "background," I mean both work experience and educational background. Again, **this depends on what angle you used in your CV.** You need to make sure to work off that angle and write both your CV and cover letter in the same light.

In real life, it means that if you have based your suitability for the role on education, you need to also reflect it in your cover letter. Do not write 5 sentences about your unrelated work experience if you presented something completely different in your CV.

With the cover letter, you are also **setting expectations for the reader.** Your cover letter needs to be intriguing enough for the reader to want to open your CV. If you do not arouse interest with your cover letter, there are very good chances the reader will not even open your CV. Your cover letter serves as an intro to your CV. It is like a movie **teaser** before the movie **trailer** is released. So, if you want someone to read the opening section of your CV that serves as a trailer, you need to have a good teaser first.

***

Here is a suggestion as to how to organize a cover letter:

- **Address the reader** – if you know the recruiter's or hiring manager's name, definitely use it. If you do not know who will be reading your job application, go with the standard **"To Whom It May Concern."**

- In the **opening paragraph,** you should explain why you think you fit the role in a few sentences. Always refer to the job ad and try to connect your background and personality to the job itself.
  A few examples would be:
  "After seeing the job ad for the role of a Store Manager, I knew I had to apply. I really found myself in the description, and I am sure our collaboration would be mutually beneficial thanks to my rich experience in the retail sector."

"I wish to apply for the position at your company because I truly believe that my positive attitude, willingness to help out a teammate, and quick learning abilities make me the perfect candidate for the role."

"I would like to apply for a job position at your company. I truly believe my educational background, willingness to learn, and hands-on experience in the world of finance and accounting meet the criteria outlined in the job post. I would really love to get an opportunity to be a part of your team!"

- The **first paragraph should follow your CV** – it can be about education, skills, or work experience. You need to link one of those segments with the job ad and convince the reader you fit the role. You already know how to do this because we have discussed it in the CV writing part.

  A few examples would be:

  "I am a formally educated Food Technician, with knowledge of production processes and technology, safety and health policies, as well as food components and the fundamentals, mechanisms, and operations of human metabolism."

"I hold a Master's and Bachelor's Degree in Business Economics with a specialization in International Business. Due to that, I have acquired knowledge of micro and macroeconomics, international trade policies, risk management, and I can solve high-level finance-related issues."

"Throughout my career, I have worked for well-established hotel chains and resorts as a digital marketing expert. Thanks to that, I am proficient in managing marketing channels and allocating budgets, running successful ad campaigns on social media, and collecting and interpreting data. I have learned how to adjust marketing and promotional activities to achieve maximum ROI and track performance."

- The **second paragraph** should reflect your **personality** – it is always good to add some "soft skills" or personality traits. Ideally, you will incorporate phrases from the job ad itself and use this paragraph to show why you are a great candidate.

    A few examples would be:

"Thanks to my rigorous attention to detail and curiosity, I have managed to track the workload of onsite teams, pinpoint quiet periods, and find creative solutions to utilize their downtime. Due to my excellent communication skills, I am able to get different teams to collaborate and think of tasks."

"I possess excellent attention to detail, analytical, problem-solving, and researching skills, which make me thorough and effective in content review. I handle pressure extremely well, mostly due to my experience in customer-focused environments in the hospitality industry. I can communicate clearly and concisely, adapt to team dynamics, and follow company and industry guidelines."

"I am detail-oriented, organized, discrete, and trustworthy. I have experience in handling sensitive and confidential data, working in a team and under pressure, and I adapt easily. I understand the importance of following protocols and keeping accurate records, and I enjoy sorting files and updating databases."

- The **third paragraph** should explain why you are **interested** in the role – you need to be honest because it will come up at the job interview.

Everyone wants to know your motivation. Why do you want to leave your current company? Why are you willing to relocate? Why are you switching careers? Of course, when I say "be honest," do not be *too* honest and state your current company is paying you peanuts. Tone it down a bit and use a business-appropriate version.

A few examples would be:

"Even though I enjoy my time in the world of localization, I feel like it is time for me to go back to something more creative and design-related. I am skilled in Photoshop, Illustrator, Sketchbook, and Autodesk Maya software with emphasis on 3D animation, and I would love to work with creative people and coordinate promotional artwork and operational activities."

"I would really like to move more in the direction of data analytics because that is my field of interest. I am sure I would contribute to the effectiveness of your team due to my work ethics and skills I possess."

"I am extremely responsible and enthusiastic about nursing, and I am looking for a more challenging position than I currently hold. I am sure that my approach to work and highly developed nursing skills would benefit your team greatly. I would love to be in an environment that motivates me to learn and develop, both professionally and personally."

- The **fourth paragraph** should be the **closing** one – in it, share your excitement about the role. Perhaps even repeat your best points that fit the job ad. That way, you are sure that, even if the person is just skimming through the cover letter, they will see the most important phrases.
A few examples would be:
"I honestly believe I could contribute to the effectiveness of your team due to my dedication and hard work. I am sure I would create a pleasant and productive work atmosphere for all involved parties.
I would greatly appreciate it if I could present my experience in more detail over the phone or a video call."

"If you are looking for an experienced and dedicated professional who cares deeply about a job well done, please, get in touch at your earliest convenience. I would love to go over my experience in more detail and discuss this amazing opportunity."

"I am extremely interested in joining your team of experts and expanding my knowledge. I would love to go over my suitability and motivation for the role in more detail. I am looking forward to your reply, and I hope to hear from you soon."

- **Sign off** the cover letter with an appropriate phrase – you can choose whichever you want, there is plenty of them, for example, "Yours Sincerely" or "Kind Regards." Also, remember to sign it.

***

So, to conclude, your cover letter needs to follow your CV. This means that if you write several versions of a CV, you need to write **several versions of a cover letter.**

Of course, write one as a base, but remember: **there should not be discrepancies between a CV and a cover letter.** It does not send a positive message.

Always align the structure of your cover letter to the CV you are using for your job application.

***

The same logic that applies to CVs applies to cover letters as well: **the most effective cover letter is the one focused on a particular job ad – tailored.**

Even if your CV is not *that* specific, you should make your cover letter as specific as possible. After all, if you are applying, you have the job ad in front of you. So, you are able to customize it and make sure it fits the job ad. If you fail to do it, you might be perceived as careless, passive, or uninterested.

7.3. THE LAYOUT OF A COVER LETTER

Now that you know what you need to write and how to organize it, let's look at the layout of a cover letter itself.

Of course, you will write your cover letter in the same word processor as your CV, and you will follow pretty much the same principle while writing it.

Your cover letter needs to be clear, tidy, pleasant to the eye, and without any distractions. Just like your CV!

Use the same font type, size, color, and spacing as you used in your CV. This shows you are consistent and have an eye for details.

Avoid any elements that can distract the reader from the content of your letter.

Separate the paragraphs and make sure everything is nicely aligned. It has to be pleasant to the eye and not look cluttered.

If you are **applying through a system that asks you to attach a separate document**, then simply upload your document.

***

If you are **applying via email**, you do not have to worry about the layout too much. Copy-paste what you had written in your document. Make sure there is **enough space between the paragraphs** and that it looks **presentable** in an email.

I would suggest sending yourself an email with your cover letter first. That way, you will see exactly what the recipient sees. Maybe you can bold super important information or add more spaces, but that should be done in moderation so the reader is not put off.

***

If you are **applying via job boards** that have their own **online forms** or via **the company's recruitment suite**, the only thing you need to worry about is **that the paragraphs are distributed correctly.**

Copy-paste what you had written in your document, and make sure to hit that "Enter" button, so your cover letter does not look too cluttered. Separate the paragraphs so that your note (cover letter) looks neat and tidy.

8. A QUICK OVERVIEW OF WHAT YOU'VE LEARNED

If you are ever in a hurry and want a rough summary of this Guide, or you'd like to remind yourself of the most important steps you need to write a successful CV and a cover letter, the below should help!

8.1. CV WRITING STEPS

- List all your skills
- List all your past positions
- List all your educational background, courses, and training sessions
- Find out what you want to do next & why
- Pinpoint how you match your desired position (skills, work experience, and/or educational background)
- Focus your CV on the points that make you a great candidate for the role

8.2. CV AND COVER LETTER WRITING TIPS

- Do not use templates
- List the most important (relevant) information first
- Do not overuse business-related terms (jargon)
- Use standard font type, size, colors, and spacing

- Incorporate keywords from job ads in your content (but do not list them in a separate section)
- Leave out any information that does not bring value (does not help to prove you are a great candidate for the role)
- Proofread your CV and cover letter

8.3. JOB SEARCH TIPS

- Tailor your CV to every job ad (position) you are applying to (to increase chances of success)
- Align your cover letter with the CV you are using for the application
- Ensure there are no huge discrepancies between your CVs and social media profiles
- Keep track of which CV and cover letter you used for which job ad
- Even when you get a job, keep your CV and cover letter updated and give it a read every few months

9. DIVE INTO JOB SEARCH (FAREWELL)

Well, this is it. We have come to the end of the road.

I have shared everything you need to know to write a winning, top-notch CV and a cover letter. :)

You are now ready to tackle the task of CV and cover letter writing, and you can take your career to a new level.

My goal was to help you see CV writing and job search in general in a new light. And to help you get a job interview. If you follow this Guide, **you will get reactions to your job applications** and, moreover, you will see impressive results!

The principles outlined in this Guide are the very same Linking Lines as a professional CV writing business uses. My clients have amazing results, and now, thanks to this step-by-step Guide, you can have the same results as well.

However, if the Guide is not enough and you feel like you are stuck in your job search, reach out to me via email at info@linkinglines.com, and I will be more than happy to help!

Best of luck in your job search adventures, may this Guide serve you well.

10. ABOUT THE AUTHOR

Due to my love of writing and research, I was encouraged to start a CV writing business. That was in September 2015, and it was predominately for immigrants wanting to move to the Republic of Ireland. That is how Linking Lines was born.

I completed several courses and became a certified Resume Writer and a Career Coach. I regularly test my own advice by sprucing up my CV and cover letter and by applying to jobs. This practical experience is how I stay on top of the game; I follow global trends and tweak Linking Lines' writing strategy as needed.

I have employed thousands of clients within various EU countries, the UK, Australia, Canada, and the USA. It gives me great satisfaction to know I've improved someone's life. My clients are from all walks of life, and the success of each one of them I celebrate as if it was my own.

Through Linking Lines, I have the opportunity to build and strengthen personal brands, encourage indecisive individuals, and help people see how great they are and what they can do! My work brings a ray of hope for a better future, and I get to participate in marvelous career adventures. As a CV writer and a career coach, I don't *just* secure job interviews. And that is my motivation for learning; that is what keeps me going!

Printed in Great Britain
by Amazon